The Unknown Pastels

Cover (Plate 1):
Boat Landing, Nahant, Massachusetts, dated 1910 on reverse
13¾" × 19⅞"

The Unknown Pastels
Maurice Brazil Prendergast

November 4th to December 5th, 1987

Coe Kerr Gallery
49 East 82nd Street New York

Universe / Coe Kerr Gallery
New York

Published in the United States of America
in 1987 by Universe Books
381 Park Avenue South, New York, N.Y. 10016

© 1987 by Coe Kerr Gallery

87 88 89 90 / 10 9 8 7 6 5 4 3 2 1

Printed in Hong Kong

ISBN 0-87663-534-6

Design: Marcus Ratliff Inc., New York
Typesetting: Trufont Typographers, Inc., New York

Foreword

In the spring of 1987, Mrs. Charles Prendergast showed Donna Seldin and me a remarkable collection of pastels that were done around the time of the First World War by her brother-in-law, Maurice Brazil Prendergast. It was a revelation to see them all together. It was known that he "dabbled" in pastel, but it was not known that he produced a distinct body of work in this medium. But more than being simply in another medium, these pastels were strikingly beautiful. They achieved an aesthetic effect far different from the watercolors and the oils of the same period. Our immediate thought was that in this medium, the artist seemed to synthesize the fluidity and clarity of watercolor with the density and impasto of oil, thereby gaining a new and quite different effect.

We felt these remarkable and unheralded works should be seen. Thanks to Mrs. Prendergast's foresight and generosity, we are thrilled to present to the public for the first time an entire exhibition of *The Unknown Pastels*.

Warren Adelson, Director
Coe Kerr Gallery

The Unknown Pastels by Maurice Brazil Prendergast

Maurice Prendergast worked in pastel for about ten years. He only exhibited them once, and this was at the end of his work in the medium. He showed four pastels at the Pennsylvania Academy 16th Watercolor Annual (November 10-December 15, 1918), and these are the only pastels known to have been exhibited. (He may have exhibited others in exhibitions where the medium was not so carefully identified.) The four works in the Pennsylvania show were always thought of as oddities, experiments by an artist who constantly experimented. Occasionally one would see a pastel in a museum or a private collection, and generally they were described as mixed media, owing to the fact that the pastel is usually applied over an understructure of watercolor. There has never been a sense that these pictures represent a distinct body of work, a coherent and prolonged effort in another medium. In fact, that is just what these pastels are: a separate body of work, distinct from the watercolors, monotypes, and oils.

Commencing in about 1910, Prendergast began to work in this very delicate medium. He had done a few tentative works in the late 1890s, but his second attempt at pastel was sustained and clearly directed: it lasted a decade. For Prendergast, pastel was not an experiment, it was a tool. It was a new tool to implement new ideas. As he had worked at monotype for a decade (the 1890s), so would he work in pastel, with dedication and a specific aesthetic intention. Some he did over existing watercolors. Perhaps they were even slightly earlier watercolors. For others he used a pencil base or pencil and watercolor base as the understructure. And still others are pure pastel. The important issue is that when he uses pastel, whether alone or in mixed media, the effect is distinctly different from the watercolors and oils of the period. The pastels have their own place within the late (or mature) period and were produced as a natural development in the evolution of those works.

Prendergast's oeuvre falls roughly into two periods, early and late. These periods conveniently divide at the turn of the century. His early works can rightfully be thought of as nineteenth century in spirit, and his late or so-called mature production, twentieth century. The distinction between these two periods is easily seen and critical to our discussion.

Prendergast was born in 1859 and grew up in Boston. His youth was marked by poverty, and it is because of this that his professional training as an artist commenced at a relatively late age. He went to Europe to study at the Académie Julian in 1892, when he was thirty-three years old, at an age more common to a

Fig. 1
Maurice Prendergast
Piazza San Marco, Venice, 1899
Watercolor on paper
19⅜" × 14¼"
Alice M. Kaplan (photo courtesy
 of Coe Kerr Gallery)

teacher than a student. An unrealized advantage of this late start was his clear predisposition toward certain art forms, an aesthetic developed by his early employment as what today would be called a graphic artist. He was immediately put off by the staid academic training and instantly drawn to all that was new in Paris in the early 1890s. It is significant to remember that he was a mature man, not an impressionable youth. His mind and his choices as an artist were very much his own. Through his new friend and fellow-student, the Canadian James Wilson Morrice, Prendergast met other avant-garde, English-speaking artists. He was subsequently introduced to a vast array of modern art, including the works of Bonnard, Vuillard, and others of the emerging Nabis group, whose beginnings were likewise at the Académie Julian. This early exposure was to dominate his choice of subjects, working methods, and artistic taste for the rest of his life.

His second European trip brought him to Venice in 1898, and notably, to the murals of Vittore Carpaccio. That sixteenth-century artist's love of the pictorial, his architectural sense, and rigorous perspective, his exuberance for pageantry and procession, his quick observation, accurate sense of gesture and pose, all enlivened with fanciful and exotic flora and fauna, costume and prop, dovetailed magically into

Prendergast's own love of the pictorial. For the next thirty years, all parasols, balloons, goats, dogs, hybrid creatures and hobbyhorses are expressions of this same taste. Carpaccio made it all possible. The minutiae of Prendergast's crowd scenes in Venice and Capri, Central Park and Revere Beach all drew inspiration from this source.

A fine example of these early works is *Piazza San Marco, Venice* (Fig. 1). Notable in this picture is the realistic progression into the deep space of the piazza, classically delineated by the intersecting lines of the pavement. Beautifully rendered are the dappled colors of the finely articulated figures and their sparkling reflections in the wet pavement. The complex design of the Byzantine architecture is carefully delineated. The same carefully constructed space and wonderfully varied and articulated figures are seen in *Monte Pincio, Rome* (Fig. 2). Few details are left to the imagination; the imagery is carefully defined and delicately painted. The space is constructed along the diagonals of the ramps, realistically leading our eye back to the upper level of figures, aided by the vertical thrusts of the trees and the statue.

Back in America, he continued painting in this essentially realistic manner. *May Day, Central Park*, 1901 (Fig. 3) has all the detailed complexity, fine articulation, and realistically rendered space of the Venetian scenes. We see the same well-dressed strollers, girls with ribbons, ladies with parasols, and the added bit of

Fig. 2
Maurice Prendergast
Monte Pincio, Rome, 1898–99
Watercolor on paper
15¼″ × 19⅜″, 43.1982
Daniel J. Terra Collection, Terra
   Museum of American Art,
   Chicago

Fig. 3
Maurice Prendergast
May Day, Central Park, c. 1901
Watercolor on paper
14½" × 21⅝"
Collection of Whitney Museum
  of American Art, New York.
  Exchange

local color, the maypole dance. It was in this essentially realistic style that Prendergast worked, principally in watercolor and monotype, through the turn of the century.

Prendergast's retrospective exhibition of sixty-four watercolors and monotypes in 1902 at the Cincinnati Museum Association can be seen as a turning point. This was the last time that he exhibited either medium as a group. Within the next few years his work changed. It was during the years 1903–4 that he began to work seriously in oil, a medium that he had worked with in the 1890s, but only in diminutive size (*pochades*, small panels). It was in oil that he began to experiment relentlessly. He reworked canvasses endlessly, having several in progress at the same time. *Central Park in 1903* (Metrolitan Museum of Art, New York) was still being worked on in 1915.

The artist was moving toward a more abstract style, moving from the pictorial to the abstract. Figurative scenes that had been objective and specific (Central Park, Piazza San Marco) now became abstractions of those scenes. They were now increasingly unspecific in locale; they became an idyllic place, a never-never land. This effect was accomplished stylistically. Brush strokes took on a decorative function; they related less clearly to the object defined. Space was no longer defined by traditional perspective. The distinction between figure and ground became hazier as they began to integrate. Form began to be defined by contour lines of contrasting hues, in effect outlining. *The Opal Sea* (Fig. 4) is a prime example of this transitional phase. This picture was executed c. 1903–6. (The date is based on contemporary documentation; the painting is not dated.) This shore scene has the realistic format of a foreground with figures that recede in space, a middle ground of the sea with boats, and the background of distant hills and a tiny ship on the horizon. The deep, convincing space and realistic lighting look back to the earlier period, as does the impressionistic blending of strokes. The figures are outlined, yet they are insubstantial; they lack the solidity and the sense of reality that we saw in the earlier crowd scenes. Here, they blend into the ground and integrate with the landscape.

Over the next decade, the demands of representation gave way to the artist's clear delight in making patterns and arabesques of color, shape, and movement. By the time he exhibited at Macbeth Gallery in 1908 at the infamous show of *The Eight,* the critics described his paintings as "a jumble of riotous pigment" and "an explosion in a color factory."

Prendergast's visit to Europe in 1907, after an absence of almost ten years, had been a revelation. The previous few years (1905–6) had been difficult. His deafness, which had been in evidence earlier, was now taking on more serious dimensions. His self-prescribed cure of sunbathing and swimming from March through November (an odd regimen) was not working. He was growing isolated by his deafness and probably as much so by his own unsure groping as an artist. He produced almost nothing during these two years. But the trip to France lifted his spirits. His notebooks of the trip are filled with notations about Giotto, Titian, Puvis de Chavannes, Van Gogh, Gauguin, Matisse, Dufy, Signac, and Roussel. But most of all, he was struck by the watercolors of Cézanne, which were on exhibition at Galérie Bernheim-Jeune in Paris. He loved them for their simplicity and suggestive qualities; he felt that "he (Cézanne) left everything

Fig. 4
Maurice Prendergast
Opal Sea, 1903–10
Oil on canvas
22″ × 34″, 30.1980
Daniel J. Terra Collection, Terra
    Museum of American Art,
    Chicago

Fig. 5
Maurice Prendergast
St. Malo No. 2, c. 1907
Watercolor on paper
12¾" × 19¼"
Columbus Museum of Art, Ohio,
    Gift of Ferdinand Howald, 1931

to the imagination." It was as much this concept as it was Cézanne's technique that affected Prendergast. In addition, he would have felt a kinship with the festival flags and striped tents of Dufy and Marquet, and he could revel in the pure color and black outlines of Vlaminck and Rouault. He was caught up in the Fauve spirit. It is no wonder that the critics of 1908 were so astonished and baffled by his works. They had never seen anything like them.

In 1909 Maurice Prendergast was fifty years old and almost completely deaf. He went to Europe again that year and renewed his contact with French painting. Much was new, and much he cast aside. He did draw from Signac the pointillist technique that artist evolved from Seurat. Noteworthy are a group of watercolors done in St. Malo in 1910 (Fig. 5). They differ radically from Prendergast's early, realistic works. The drawing is freer, the value contrasts sharper, and the colors more brilliant and fauve-like. The brushwork is rectangular, reminiscent of the scientific impressionism of Seurat, but without its cold order or chromatic logic. Prendergast's color is spontaneous, not calculated.

Done also in 1910 is the first of our pastels, *Boat Landing, Nahant, Massachusetts* (Plate 1) which is dated 1910 on the reverse. It represents a day of leisure, with figures casually grouped, lounging on the grass, walking arm in arm. Some look out to the bright blue sea, white sails, and purple hills beyond. There is a mood of serenity tinged with nostalgia. Its resemblance in composition and theme to Seurat's masterpiece *A Sunday Afternoon on the Island of La Grande Jatte,* 1884–86 (The Art Institute of Chicago) cannot be coincidental. However, the pastel is pure Prendergast. Stylistically the scene is still representational. Like the St. Malo watercolors (Fig. 5) and oils like *The Opal Sea* (Fig. 4), the figures in the pastel are defined in space. The pier in the middle ground is convincingly rendered, and the distant hills are diminished by aerial perspective. However, by using the unique qualities of the pastel the figures blend into the ground, and the brushwork (the working of the pastel stick) creates a uniform surface, thereby integrating the entire surface of the picture. The figures and the rather magical trees set up a rhythm, an almost serpentine movement across the paper. This surface harmony is heightened by the intense color, brighter even than the St. Malo watercolors. It is the pure color of the pastel stick, unblended, undiluted by oil or water medium. Moreover, the pastel is applied over a base of watercolor, which by its nature is transparent. The combination of transparent watercolor overlaid with opaque chalk creates a startling chromatic effect. The color is not just brighter, it has a density, a richness, a texture that is startling. It has a surface texture without the thickness or opacity of oil paint. Thus it is both translucent and impastoed. There is produced a suffused, shadowless radiance, a luminous effect that records not the effect of light on color, but pure color untouched by light.

Another pastel done in Nahant and probably in 1910 is *Road to the Beach, Nahant* (Plate II). The artist returns to an old theme but treats it in a new manner. How different this is from the 1901 watercolor of the same theme in the Whitney Museum (Fig. 3). In the pastel one has to look carefully to discern figure from ground from tree. The maypole is apparent when one looks for it, but hardly a focal point, as it is in the Whitney picture. The crowd size is greatly diminished in number in the pastel. It is more emblematic, a symbol of a crowd, or, more accurately, an abstraction of a crowd. The pastel colors have a purity and a density lacking in the early watercolor. Moreover there is a boldness of brushwork, almost a bravura quality to the handling of the medium, much like the paint surface of the oils.

The dating of the pastels is as baffling and elusive as the chronology of the oils and monotypes. In his essay for the 1960 Boston Museum exhibition catalogue, Hedley Howell Rhys called dating the undated oils "a hazardous procedure." Cecily Langdale said that dating the monotypes is "educated conjecture" (*Monotypes by Maurice Prendergast in the Terra Museum of American Art*). Likewise the chronology of the pastels is difficult. But one can draw some conclusions. There are at least two others that seem to relate to the 1910 date in our group. They are *The Pavilion* (Plate III) and *Girls on the Riverbank* (Plate IV). Both have figures of the same scale as Plates I and II. They are arranged thoughtfully in relation to the forms of the trees around and above them. They are all roughly the same paper size, and the application of the pastel, the definition of form, and the number and arrangement of the figures are all similar. Based on that, one could tentatively place these four works at the 1910 date.

After returning from Europe in 1912, Prendergast was asked to be on both the foreign and American selection committees for the forthcoming Armory Show. This was a telling honor. By now he was recognized as America's leading "modern" painter. With his usual modesty, he chose only seven of his own works for the exhibition. Among the buyers of his work in the show were Mrs. John Kraushaar and his

Fig. 6
Maurice Prendergast
Massachusetts Shore
Watercolor and pastel on paper
13⅜" × 19¼"
Photo courtesy of Columbus
    Museum of Art, Ohio

dear friend William Glackens. In the following year, 1914, Maurice and his brother, Charles, finally quit Boston after over five decades of living there, and moved to 50 Washington Square, New York, a building also occupied by Glackens and considered to be the center of the art world. War-time New York was certainly the center of all domestic and European avant-garde art, housing galleries and attracting collectors from all over the country. Ample proof of this was the stunning success of his exhibition at the Carroll Gallery in February 1915. On view were sixty oils and watercolors of the past eight years. It was an art dealer's dream: a feeding frenzy among collectors. Supposedly John Quinn and Dr. Albert Barnes practically came to blows over who would get first choice to purchase Prendergasts. The move to New York and the European war had another effect: travel was limited to this country. Prendergast's pattern for his remaining years was to be winters in New York, working in the studio on oils, and summers traveling in New England, working out of doors in watercolor and pastel.

A complete log of his summer sojourns is not known. Hedley Howell Rhys, in his essay for the 1960 catalogue, listed the following: 1915, Annisquam; 1916, 1917, Nahant, Swampscott; 1918, 1919, Salem; 1915, 1919, 1920, Gloucester; 1922, Marblehead. The pastel entitled *Gloucester* (Plate XI) is dated 1915 on the reverse. From this piece, we may attempt to link a few other pastels to that date based on stylistic similiarities. *Gloucester* is very freely stroked, the figures having an almost rubbery quality, posed in doll-like fashion in a pictorially rendered shore setting. The sailboat in the water and the groups of houses on the distant shore are rendered with some sense of aerial perspective, and thus recede realistically in space. The color is even brighter and more pure than the 1910 pastels. *Rockport* (Plate XII) and *Gloucester* (Plate XI) are done on sheets about the same size, have the same rag-doll figures, sweeping brushwork, and bright color. It is a good guess that these were done around the 1915 date. Likewise two landscapes without figures of the same locale entitled *Gloucester* (Plate XIV) and *House with Flag in the Cove* (Plate XV) appear to be 1915. Their brushwork has the same easy flow and free form as the works discussed above. Moreover, the somewhat realistic perspective and definition of space precludes a later date.

Salem (Plate XVI) and *Folly Cove, Gloucester* (Plate XVII) were probably done around 1915. They relate closely to *Massachusetts Shore* (Fig. 6), a pastel of the same size, subject, handling, and compositional formula. This piece was purchased by one of the artist's greatest collectors of the period, Ferdinand Howald. Mr. Howald, whose collection later went to the Columbus Museum, purchased this piece from the Daniel Gallery in 1921.

At some time after the Armory Show (1913), Prendergast started to paint large figures in seashore settings. Many of these works he titled generically "cove" or "promenade." It was this theme, which in fact was rooted in his early crowd scenes, that he repeated constantly. It was the vehicle for his statement: color and design. These pieces grew from numerous sources artistically, including Cézanne, Denis, and Roussel, and from the entirety of his experience as an artist. They are the apotheosis of Prendergast's modernism. They are the least realistic, the most abstract, and the most daring of all of his work. They range from figures in

Fig. 7
Maurice Prendergast
Swampscott Beach, c. 1917
Watercolor, graphite, gouache and
    pastel on paper
15⅝" × 22¹/₁₆"
The Carnegie Museum of Art,
    Pittsburgh; Gift of Edward Duff
    Balken, 1949

Fig. 8
Maurice Prendergast
Outer Harbor
Oil on panel
18½" × 32¼"
Private collection (photo courtesy
  of Coe Kerr Gallery)

a discernable setting (coves with headland and finger outlets) to figures formally arranged against an abstracted background. *A Day of Leisure* (Plate XVIII) and *Holiday* (Plate XIX) represent a variety of figures playing by the shore. Some of the women have the elegant, attenuated bodies and small heads of sixteenth-century mannerist art. The figure sizes vary less because of the height of the individuals or their being seen in perspective, but rather due to the artist's arbitrary arrangement on the paper. The foreground space is not possible; impossibly tall and short figures are compressed as if between glass. They move, gyrate, and wiggle in a world of their own. In *Holiday* (Plate XIX), the figures in the cove integrate with the rocks and shore, and some can barely be discerned from the ground. A nude is practically disguised in the foreground before our eyes, and her mirror image has been all but obliterated to the right. The headland and houses and water in both pastels seem stacked atop the compositions. We intellectually understand what and where they are, but we do not read them by traditional perspective. They are part of the entire fabric of the surface of the paper, built by layered patterns of tightly stitched brushwork. The brushwork of the underlying watercolor and the surface harmony of the pastel create an interwoven fabric that we read all at once. *Swampscott Beach* (Fig. 7) is a pastel in the collection of the Museum of Art, Carnegie Institute (Pittsburgh). It appears to be the same location as *Holiday* and includes the same attenuated, mannered figures dressed in similiar costumes as both of our pastels. The date of the Carnegie picture is listed as 1916, and this seems a likely date for our two.

Bathers, New England (Plate XX) is the largest and most densely packed figure composition in the pastel group. Like the above-mentioned two pastels, it is a compression of elongated and abbreviated figures arranged in a shore setting. Here, however, the figures are more posed, more self-consciously grouped than the two discussed above. There is a sense of the casual, perhaps random crowd in *Holiday* and *A Day of Leisure*, but not so in *Bathers, New England*. The composition is formal; both sides are flanked by seated women in bathing suits with other standing and seated figures behind them, enclosing or encircling the group. To the right is what Prendergast called the "good figure." The featureless, monumental woman in the orange coat acts as an anchor, a focal point to give rhythm and direction to the composition. The water and signature headland are woven into the design of the picture by their brushwork and serve as a backdrop, a screen for the figures. The fluidity of the watercolor is given density by the rich pastel. The surface has a dry, scumbled effect, much like the oils of this late period. We see that same arid, impastoed effect in *Outer Harbor* (Fig. 8). This is a typical cove composition, the carefully arranged figures woven across the tightly compressed foreground. The figure placement is deliberate, contrived for artistic ends. A pastel in the Museum of Fine Arts, Boston, entitled *Maine Beach, Late Afternoon* (Fig. 9) is a shore scene similar to *Bathers, New England*. The Boston picture is dated 1916, which seems apt for our piece.

Of the late pastels, the most daring are *Distance Hills, Maine* (Plate XXI) and *On the Rocks, North Shore* (Plate XXII). Here we see the artist at his most abstract. We are far away from the piazzas of Venice and the parks of New York. These bathing scenes are arabesques of the imagination, voyages into an interior world. The figures are synthetically proportioned to occupy a designed space. In *On the Rocks, North Shore* we can discern the rocks and the water, but they are more emblems of those elements than the real stuff. The design of the water brings to mind those contrivances of Hokusai, not the crashing surf of Gloucester. The figures have a monumentality, as though they were extracted from antiquity, yet there is no sense of reality. They weave in and out of the design of the rocks and water as though they were made of the same material.

Fig. 9
Maurice Prendergast
Maine Beach, Late Afternoon, c. 1916
Pastel
14¾″ × 21¾″
Courtesy, Museum of Fine Arts,
    Boston, Abraham Schuman Fund.

Distance Hills, Maine is an abstraction done late in this body of work. Nude and clothed women, arbitrarily sized, are paraded before us on the artist's stage. An unlikely deer is petted by the seated nude in the center. A red parasol floats over the head of the woman to the right. It is the same red parasol that floats overhead in *Picnic Grove* (Fig. 10), the 1918 oil in the Museum of Fine Arts, Boston. Here too is a proscenium of women, artfully arranged and enveloped by the deep green of the unarticulated foliage. In both works, the red parasol serves as an element of design in the composition as well as a chromatic counterpoint to the green of the oil and the purple of the pastel. Both paintings, oil and pastel, have the same dry, textured surface, sense of overall design, and luscious color harmonies.

By 1922, Prendergast's health began to fail. He did not go to New England the following year. He exhibited in numerous museum and gallery shows and was awarded several prizes. He died, as he had lived, peacefully on February 1, 1924.

Warren Adelson
July, 1987

Plates

All of the works are pastel or pastel and watercolor on paper;
media are discussed in the body of the text. The dimensions are
listed in inches with the vertical given first. The titles given
are as inscribed on the reverse of each pastel by the artist or
other hands. We have reproduced these pastels in our sense of
the chronological order based on inscribed dates on reverse and
stylistic relationships with other works. We consider this
chronology tentative at best.

Plate I
Boat Landing, Nahant, Massachusetts, dated 1910 on reverse
13¾" × 19⅞"

Plate II
Road to the Beach, Nahant, c. 1910
12″ × 17⅞″

Plate III
The Pavilion, c. 1910
13⅞" × 19⅞"

Plate IV
Girls on the Riverbank, c. 1910
12⅛" × 17⅞"

Plate V
Naples, c. 1910
$12\frac{1}{4}'' \times 19''$

Plate VI
Farm on the Bay, c. 1910–15
12″ × 17¾″

Plate VII
Siesta, c. 1910–15
11″ × 13¼″

Plate VIII
Picking Strawberries, c. 1910–15
11″ × 13⅜″

Plate IX
Landscape with Figures and Goat, c. 1910–15
12" × 17⅞"

Plate X
Farmhouse in New England, c. 1915
19⅞″ × 13⅞″

Plate XI
Gloucester, dated 1915 on reverse
11″ × 15½″

Plate XII
Rockport, c. 1915
13¾" × 16⅜"

Plate XIII
Gloucester, c. 1915
12″ × 18″

Plate XIV
Gloucester, c. 1915
$11\frac{1}{4}''$ × $15\frac{1}{2}''$

Plate XV
House with Flag in the Cove, c. 1915
13⅞" × 20⅛"

Plate XVI
Salem, c. 1915
12″ × 18″

Plate XVII
Folly Cove, Gloucester, c. 1915
14″ × 19⅞″

Plate XVIII
A Day of Leisure, c. 1916
12⅛″ × 18⅞″

Plate XIX
Holiday, c. 1916
14¼" × 22⅜"

Plate XX
Bathers, New England, c. 1916
15⅛″ × 22½″

Plate XXI
Distance Hills, Maine, c. 1918
13¾″ × 19⅞″

Plate XXII
On the Rocks, North Shore, c. 1918
13⅞" × 19⅞"